Mourning Cloak

Poems by

Selma Mann

Sept. 4, 2013
To Marlene :)
I wish you days filled with laughter, love and butterflies.
Enjoy!
Selma

Mourning Cloak

Poems by

Selma Mann

Première

Sortie

Première Sortie Press
P.O. Box 13279
Newport Beach, CA 92658

© 2013 by Selma Mann
All rights domestic and international retained by the author.
Published 2013
First Edition

ISBN: 978-0-9897515-0-6

Library of Congress Control Number: 2013914303

Printed in the U.S.A.

*To Al Mann, my Love,
with gratitude for over 40 years together.*

Contents

Photographs	11
Foreword	13
Preface	15
With Thanks	18
Love and loss	19
Nightmare	21
Imagining Al describing his last day	23
Old souls and butterflies	25
Final journey	27
Circle of love	29
Crap and butterflies	31
Fog creeps in	33
Oh crap	35
Peace	37
Roller coaster	39
Miracles	41
Grasping for bearings	43
Missing you	45
I don't miss you	47
Acting as if . . .	49
Family	51
Inner hermit	53
Clouds	55
Chocolate grief	57

Bearings lost and found	59
The morning you were alive	61
Coming down with grief	63
One-armed man	65
Girl grief	67
My mother	69
Mining for self	71
Juggling	73
Fear is not my friend	75
Poems, poems everywhere	77
Trolling for butterflies	79
Ode to Donovan	81
Just a walk	83
Impatience	85
My muse	87
You can't force butterflies	89
Flashback	91
My breasts and I	93
My breasts	95
Anxiety	99
Just routine	101
Hospital bracelet	103
Final surgery	105
Homecoming	107
Tightrope	109

Back on the edge	111
Good samaritan	113
How could it be?	115
At peace	117
Flying to Cindy	119
ICU	121
Eli	123
Forget Houdini	125
Ending	127
Grief on my sleeve	129
Transformations	131
Wonder	133
Transformation	135
Odd	137
Falling	139
Grief again	141
The care of love	143
Dreaming	145
Earring	147
Putter	149
Folding laundry	151
Passport	153
Beautiful baby girl	155
Creation	157
Edge	159
About the poet	161

Photography credits

Selma Mann   Cover "Lanakai Rainbows"
                 page 142 "Donovan"

Quenby Shick   page 78 "Trolling for Butterflies"
                 page 126 "Mother and Daughter"

Donovan Coleman
                 page 161 "The Poet"

Foreword

This astonishing little book of poems was not a conscious design—it just happened, as though delivered like beams of love into Selma Mann's fingertips by an insistent muse. The poems sparkle with ingenious images, artful word play, and a startling sense of reality. But there is drama in these pages if you know the bare outline of Mann's recent history.

The poet, a Loyola University-trained attorney, a rational-humanist sort—romantic and sufficiently spiritual—found herself driven to composition by the death of her husband, Al, her own struggle with breast cancer on the heels of Al's death, and her mother's slow, silent fading from existence. These changes heaped on an already full plate of matriarchal ups and downs—children, grandchildren, spouses-in-law...

In grief, pain, and poetry she discovered a world of enchantment emerging from and fusing with the natural world, rendering it a luscious, sparkling place to live, despite its sharp edges and often cruel surprises, a world perhaps directed and monitored "in a secret cave by gnomes sipping chamomile." Thus she found herself a poet by necessity. Her muse seems to act as a guardian angel, demanding poems to suit the occasion when confusion cries for understanding. When Mann wanders too deeply into the woods and feels lost, the muse forces her to find her way with her pen as a compass.

Like W.B. Yeats, also an ardent listener to muses, Selma Mann has fashioned a singular spiritual view of the world that one need not analyze to delight in and learn from.

There is drama, tragedy and comedy here, viewed from new camera angles, but also a wisdom whose price to the bearer is always dear.

J. Alexie Crane, III
Poetry Editor
Première Sortie Press
Newport Beach, California

Preface

My poetry has been a gift of loss. On January 18, 2009, Al, my soulmate for over 40 years, died. We called each other "Love," one of those couples always holding hands. I felt broken without him, but found myself comforted by an unexpected connection: the beautiful dark butterflies known as "Mourning Cloak" that appeared in my garden shortly after Al's death, flying and playing around me and those I love, landing on my hat, filling me with wonder. I'm convinced that they're tiny pieces of his spirit saying "hi."

My world had changed. I was going through the motions of returning to work, spending time with family and friends. I began attending a bereavement group that would prove to be my road back to life. Healing from the loss required that I look within in ways I never had before. But more loss lay ahead.

Nine months after finding Al's body, I was diagnosed with invasive breast cancer. Bilateral mastectomies, lymph node removal, and reconstruction followed. It was the first time in my life I'd been hospitalized for anything other than giving birth to my daughters. I devoutly hope it's the last. I missed Al. I clearly remember lying in my hospital bed frightened and in pain, when I felt a hand on my shoulder that I'm convinced was Al.

It was around this time that I found myself writing poems. I did not find my muse. My muse found me. I suddenly found myself compelled to write poems that seemed to arrive whole from someplace in my spirit I didn't know existed. I had been a logical, left-brained attorney, and until that time, my writing had consisted of legal documents.

I returned to work after my surgery only to be laid off from the job I loved. It was a devastating blow, a personal rejection, since work had been my refuge in difficult times. In hindsight, I sometimes wonder if the universe was telling me that I needed a little more time to recover and write poetry.

My poetry has evolved, although I still have no idea where the poems come from. They appear to me, usually in their entirety, often in the garden or as I'm on a walk, and I feel an urgent need to reach for my notebook or sit at a computer. I recognize they are created from fragments of my experiences since childhood, causing me to wonder where my muse was hiding all this time. I've written about grief, sorrow, love, family, and laughter. One of my earliest poems was about my breasts, describing my feelings about the mastectomies. It remains one of my favorites.

I wish I could say I'm free of sorrow, but in November I lost my beautiful, courageous mother, Carlota. This time I was blessed to be able to say goodbye. It's a very different grief journey from my previous losses.

My life is filled with love and connection, and I feel surrounded by angels and spirits. I'm studying French, and I'm sure the reason I'm doing it will eventually reveal itself, because that seems to be the way my life works these days. I'm traveling again and have discovered that I can have a lot of fun traveling on my own, even to places where I don't know anyone. It's difficult to believe that January, 2013, was the fourth anniversary of Al's death and the third anniversary of my surgery, which was also my third year free of cancer. I must confess I'm a bit of a Pollyanna, always looking for silver linings.

I have faced the events and flow of my life, and believe that no matter how dark and frightening they may be, if I keep walking I will get through them, and find unexpected gifts in their wake. I am, after all, a poet now, and a suitable landing field for butterflies.

With Thanks

I am grateful beyond words to Julius and Carlota, the remarkable parents who taught me values by example, both of whom exhibited an uncommon capacity for reinventing themselves, overcoming barriers of language and perception.

My daughters, Cindy and Laurie, never cease to surprise me, and have encouraged and loved my poetry from the beginning. My grandson Donovan, who shares my enchantment with butterflies, has given me the privilege of entry into his world.

My loving and patient friends Gail, Carol, Quenby and Caroll have been wonderful sounding boards for my poems, impatient for new ones.

My good friend Jack convinced me that I'm a poet. He has been an incredible and patient teacher, generous with his time and talent, who has expected the best from me.

And the journey might not have begun without the guidance of Marilyn Kaplan, the facilitator of the bereavement groups at Hoag Hospital, who lovingly, and with wisdom far beyond her years, was instrumental in leading me through my grief until I could recognize the gifts it had left in its wake. Finally, I must thank my muse, with her bounty and surprises, continuing to delight me with her poems. I can't imagine my life without her. I thank you all, as this book would not be a reality without you.

Love and loss

Nightmare

Waken
Sound in darkness

Water running
Stillness.

Annoyance
Not again

Light under bathroom door
Dread

Calling
No answer

Open door
Moist and warm, sauna

Horror
My love floating face down in water

Panic
Rush to turn him

Water is hot
Memories of CPR

Can't lift him
Helpless

Run to call 911
Sobbing

Run back
Fear mixed with hope

Pink and warm
cruel simulation of life

Paramedics
Big, competent, kind.

Sorry ma'am
Did what we could to revive.

Questions: pain or sudden
Drowning or suicide

World upside down
Relief, Guilt

Wrenching grief
Real.

Imagining Al describing his last day

I'm not too sure how it happened.
It was such a confusing day.
In the morning Love went to a meeting,
leaving me at Peet's on the way.

I spent some time with my buddies
at the coffee shop chewing the fat.
My thinking would go off on tangents,
good friends pulled me back where I sat.

I organized a lot of stuff
as I felt compelled to do.
I used a lot of pink stickers,
but why, I haven't a clue.

I read Mark Twain for a while
and took time to chat and to play.
Love and I talked of the future.
She was worried is all I can say.

We went to Café Panini
to order our favorite meal.
We walked holding hands and laughing.
It wasn't a very big deal.

I went right on organizing
for many more hours that night
until Love said she loved me and kissed me
went to bed and turned out the light.

The rest is surreal as it happens.
I went to the bathroom and sat.
I had taken my clothes for the next day
except for my shoes and my hat.

I really thought it was morning,
waking in the dark was my habit.
I shaved to please my Love.
The heater fell and I tried to grab it.

It tumbled into the basket
unplugging itself as it fell.
I just left it there; I was tired,
and I wasn't feeling so well.

I remembered I'd turned on the shower
which was running and hot, and filling the tub.
I reached over to pull out the stopper,
intending to give it a tug.

That's pretty much all I remember
of the moment my heart ceased to fight.
My pain and confusion were gone;
fleeting sadness, then laughter and light.

Old souls and butterflies

An old soul and a cheerful disposition
are not contradictory,
as demonstrated daily
by my youngest daughter.

The world seems brighter
in her presence,
sparkling brown eyes,
shining with intelligence and light.

Beauty with depth,
a mass of dark and curly hair,
a smile that draws you closer
to warm your heart.

I can at least attempt to describe
her positive energy:
a butterfly rainbow in a field of gratitude.
Her soul is a more challenging subject.

She faced an ordeal with courage and smiles as a child,
confessing how she managed to endure, wise beyond her years,
by repeating what became a family mantra:
"Tomorrow this will be yesterday."

Willing to love,
even if the result is pain,
she understands that life is to be lived,
undaunted in her quest to find the good.

She was at my side the night Al died,
ready to share my nightmare,
in spite of her own pain,
cradling my broken spirit as it sought escape.

The next morning, she cleaned the bathroom,
where I had found his body in the night.
She understood it was not a room to fear,
just part of a house filled with years of love and peace.

They were loving acts, performed by a grieving daughter,
for she and my love were kindred spirits from the start.
Later that day, as she and Donovan were in the garden
she received a gift of beauty in return.

A beautiful dark butterfly landed on Donovan's head,
stayed a while, then flew to rest on Laurie's.
Tears ran down her lovely face when she described it,
as she kept saying, "I know that it was Papa Al."

And so began my journey with the butterflies,
magical creatures I later learned were known as Mourning Cloak
delicate couriers of messages of love,
yet with strength to shift the axis of my soul.

Final journey

It feels like a final journey
even though you live in my heart.
Traveling with your ashes
reminds me that we're apart.

I think you sent me an angel
to put my bag in the bin.
You made sure he was handsome and strong;
as he hoisted, I could feel your grin.

It's not like our other travels,
when we snuggled and held hands,
excited as we grew closer
to distant exotic lands.

We're carrying out your wishes.
I'm sure you would rather be here.
As we scatter you among redwoods,
we'll thank you and trust you are near.

We'll be a small and caring group
remains mingled with tears, love and rain.
We know that your spirit's among us,
warm memories will soften the pain.

Circle of love

Marriage
Joined in eyes of God and family
till death do us part,
in love.

Honeymoon
hand in hand in enchanted forest
sparkling in morning mist,
like our love.

Waterfall
Regally playful in the distance
amused by radiance and certainty
of our love.

Family
Vow to cherish and honor one another
and our children
with our love.

Life
Gloriously unpredictable,
surprising with joys and sorrows
shared with love.

Death
Sudden unexpected parting,
bathed in grief
by memories of love.

Freedom
Ashes scattered among redwoods,
majestic witnesses of spirit and magic,
like our love.

Completion
Part of nature and the seasons,
fulfilling the promise
of Love.

Crap and butterflies

Fog creeps in

Fog creeps in
mortality stamps its feet.

Oh crap

I'm having an "oh crap" day
and I know why.
I guess I need a butterfly.

Peace

Leaves dancing in the wind,
butterfly waving in the breeze,
Love's caress.

Roller coaster

Roller coaster time
once meant spring in Disneyland.
When did it become winter in a world of grief?
Will the meaning change again,
like the seasons?

Miracles

I once saw an angel
above my favorite tree.
Its wings unfurled
and filled me with love and warmth and awe.

I keep looking at my tree,
though I know that seeing an angel
is not an everyday occurrence,
but I'm distracted

by butterflies,
hummingbirds,
and a perfect spider web
outlined by droplets of water.

Where is my angel?
I begin to see
that I don't choose
my miracles.

I open my eyes and my soul
to distractions.

Grasping for bearings

Missing you

I miss you in winter,
listening to rain,
snuggled like cozy spoons,
delicious in the cold.

I miss you in spring,
walking hand in hand,
as nature keeps its promise
of rebirth.

I miss you in summer,
sharing ripe and luscious fruit
you lovingly selected
at its perfect peak.

I miss you in autumn,
our favorite travel time,
adventure weather,
crisp and clear.

I don't miss you

Glancing at a couple sleeping,
snuggled like puppies
on the train,
I don't miss you.

Watching our travel buddies,
their gait adjusted
to his pain,
I don't miss you.

Noticing a couple holding hands,
across the aisle
on a plane,
I don't miss you

Knowing how much
we would have laughed
in the rain,
I don't miss you

Seeing your image beside my reflection,
reminding me that love
will remain,
I don't miss you.

You are a part of me.
Memories once heavy with sorrow,
surprise me with warmth, bearing solace.
How could I miss you?

Acting as if . . .

Family

I've found a great new family
of which I'm now a part.
There was a catch, because to join
requires a broken heart.

I lost my love, my soulmate
and saw my whole world shatter,
but the sharing in the group
helps me find new things that matter.

We never tire of hearing
stories of the ones we lost,
of our bittersweet adventures,
as our souls start to defrost.

At every new success
we clap and say "well done,"
and begin to see the future
as a place we might have fun.

There's turmoil and there's drama,
yet that's really not too bad,
because knowing life's in session
sure beats always feeling sad.

Inner hermit

I have a powerful and demanding inner hermit,
requiring abundant feedings of peace and contemplation
to recharge.

He'd have you think he's a kind and gentle roommate,
subsisting on the ultimate benevolent diet of solitude,
and yet,

he has a way of getting exactly what he needs,
releasing feelings of unease and agitation,
holding poems hostage.

In exchange, he grants glimpses of my spirit
as he woos my muse,
a fragile coexistence of respect.

Clouds

I should have been named Pollyanna,
always looking for a silver lining.
Though I'm thankful for gratitude,
sometimes I just need to sit in a cloud.

Chocolate grief

By popular demand
I'm bringing your famous brownies
to Ruth's party,

hoping that this year
I will not feel the gorge of your absence
rising through laughter and kindness.

I followed the recipe,
including every decadent ingredient,
as I recall.

I taste one to ensure its luscious heritage.
It is gloriously chocolate, after all,
and yet

I think the brownies miss you,
and the joy you brought to them,
as I do.

I go to the party
carrying the platter of brownies,
my talisman of welcome.

Bearings lost and found

The morning you were alive

Last Monday when I woke you were still alive.
Another dimension must have sneezed that day,
or it may have been a magical alignment of planets and stars.

I lay against my pillow, thinking mundane morning thoughts,
and that I needed your advice
about tax-free municipal bonds.

I remember the feeling of wholeness and satisfaction,
the security of knowing you were here,
as I surrendered to contentment.

The sensation was so real.
Till gradually, knowledge of your death crept in,
breaking into the interlude with my former self.

I was surprised by the absence of grief,
feeling gratitude
for the gift of awareness I received.

Coming down with grief

I'm coming down with grief.
My throat is tight,
eyes teary, legs weary,
achy lassitude,
heaviness I can't define.

I've had it before,
and suspect I will again.
Fortunately,
unlike the first time,
I know it will pass.

The best course of action
is to embrace it.
Avoidance intensifies the symptoms
and prolongs the pain.
Distraction kicks it down the road.

But I accept its reality
listening for its message
and sometimes, in its wake,
it leaves an unexpected gift,
maybe even a poem or two.

One-armed man

I imagine a one-armed man,
his body remembering,
eventually adapting to loss.

Losing a great love, a soulmate,
feels different.
I am learning to live without you,
but know I am missing a piece of soul.

I open my heart,
revealing the loss,
and try to recapture
wholeness.

Girl grief

Grief is like toenail fungus.
I can cover it with bright polish,
making others more comfortable,
but it will continue to grow and fester
under the pretty coating.

My mother

Shattered by grief
into thousands of tiny shards.
A kaleidoscope of loss,
reflecting bits of sorrow, pain,
regret,
and eventually, love.

Piece by piece,
beginning to arrange the chaos
into a new whole,
so different from her earlier self,
revealing gifts of spirit, laughter
and connection.

In cruel inexorable reversal,
age and dementia deconstruct
what courage and patience created,
removing memories and speech;
a hurricane inexplicably
leaving love and laughter.

Only the eyes remain
a window to her soul.
Her vulnerability frightens me.
I hold her and kiss her like a child,
thanking her for the strength of spirit
that is her legacy to me.

Mining for self

A rich vein of insecurity lives within,
concealed beneath peaks of achievement
and the variegated landscape
of friendship and love.

Ore created by feeling different, lonely, afraid,
not quite good enough,
measured by my own harsh standards,
cruel, unrealistic, and assimilated.

Held in abeyance
by feeling loved and cherished,
and by the joy of loving and cherishing
in return.

Revealed by an unexpected slight,
perceived failure, rejection or exclusion,
a sample offered to another shopper,
or, absurdly, a checkstand closing just as I arrive.

Always surprising
in its exquisite pain
when I bite into the feeling,
even as I deny its logic.

Juggling

Juggling others' fears and needs,
no matter how briefly and skillfully
I touch them,
still allows bits and pieces
to rub off on my spirit,
triggering illusions
of control.

Fear is not my friend

Fear is not my friend,
yet I welcome her to my home,
even as I realize
that no good can come of it.

She's devious
and a master of disguise,
pretending to be an urgent crisis
is a favorite tactic.

She dresses as the stock market
or violence in the Middle East.
One day she really scared me,
masquerading as Michelle Bachman.

Which explains why
I keep opening the door,
believing
it's the adult thing to do.

One of these days
I will slam the door
in her face,
even if it's rude.

If she tries to return,
I'll simply let her know
that I'd rather hang around
with Faith and Hope.

Poems, poems everywhere

Poems everywhere I look,
whenever I listen,
whatever I feel.

Where have they been,
my word friends,
now a part of my very soul.

Maybe they were hidden,
until a volcano of grief and pain
burned away the mist.

78 ❧ Selma Mann

Trolling for butterflies

Ode to Donovan

Please forgive me for being late,
I've been an eight-year-old for a week,
on Donovan-Standard-Time.

Enchanted by its magic,
I eagerly tumble under
the paradoxical spell of simplicity.

Busy exploring new places.
It's delicious to be eight
with a car and a credit card.

Going to sleep late,
complicitly succumbing
to every delightful distraction.

Sitting side-by-side in the garden
on butterfly watch,
quietly talking about our lives.

Experiencing each moment,
accepting its fragile beauty
as it passes through our day.

Just a walk

All I wanted was a quiet walk.
I tiptoed silently out of the house,
but the memories heard me,
and attached themselves to me,
clinging to my legs
as children do.

Walking faster
didn't leave them behind.
I found myself dragging
images of the past,
an unlikely
and surprisingly heavy train.

Until I slowed
and accepted them as friends.
They flew beside me then,
the past and the moment
holding hands.

Impatience

Poems inside me are bursting to come out and play,
words filled with joy, humor and absurdity.
They're trying to be patient, but it's hard
when latecomers of grief and loss
cut to the front of the line.

I thought of setting up a number system
like the ones at the deli and the post office,
but I don't think it would work.
They'll just need to work it out
among themselves.

I think they've started reconciling,
someplace within I didn't even know existed,
as I begin writing of pain and sadness,
take flight describing transformation,
and land on gratitude and laughter.

My muse

I have a muse,
unlikely as those words sound
to my logical self,
so quick to judge.

Evidence is irrefutable,
as poems gloriously
mysteriously and
unpredictably appear.

I suspect she's a woman,
requiring immediate attention.
My muse needs and deserves
to be honored.
I can't take her for granted,
and need to be careful
not to force her gifts
to please others.

I'm beginning to recognize
her moods,
opening my heart
as she illuminates my soul.

I'm filled with joy by her presence,
aware of the moment,
connected with time and spirit,
humble and grateful.

You can't force butterflies

You can't force butterflies,
mythical symbols of transformation,
eating, resting, emerging, drying their wings,
an ancient rite of eternal patience.
Gracing my garden on a whim,
even trusting my hand as a landing pad,
filling me with joy.
Ephemeral beauty concentrated
in a time-shortened universe.

Flashback

The young mother cradled
her weeks-old baby,
its tiny head
with its full head of hair
securely cradled
in the crook of her elbow.

Seemingly unaware,
she moved instinctively,
moving the small one in an ancient rhythm
as she swayed gently from side to side.
Then she yawned widely
revealing sleeplessness and love.

My breasts and I

My breasts

I've had my breasts forever,
as long as I recall,
at first just small brown circles
snug and flat on my chest wall.

Around the time of puberty
they really grew a lot.
I was bewildered and amazed.
The boys thought I was hot.

I must admit I liked the cleavage
and how good they felt to touch.
They were just the perfect size,
not too little, not too much.

When my two babies were born
a new chapter was begun,
the breasts were nourishing and nurturing,
instead of just for fun.

The years were kind and gentle.
They stayed perky with no slack,
unless, of course, I happened
to be lying on my back.

I loved them and was grateful
for the many joys they carried.
Al never ceased admiring them
the whole time we were married.

Then one sad night my true love died,
and they really missed his gaze.
They didn't like the grief world
that had filled too many days.

Another story waited.
Cancer sneaked in unannounced.
Bilateral mastectomies
would ensure it could be trounced.

The night before the surgery
I held them one by one.
I cried yet I was grateful,
for we'd had a darn good run.

For the battle to be won,
there simply was no issue.
The cancer was removed
along with my breast tissue.

New grief was layered over old,
yet step by step I walked right through,
with love and family and friends
and my soulmate's spirit too.

Sometimes it wasn't easy,
but I really hate to lose,
so I focused on the gifts,
which included my new muse.

There have been lots of poems
and butterflies galore.
My breasts don't just have implants,
they have memories, and more.

I have two lovely, perky breasts.
Barbie comes to mind;
and when I lie upon my back,
they're certainly more kind.

I'd take my old ones in a trade,
but I didn't have that choice.
So I say 'thank you,' and each day
I remember to rejoice.

❀

Anxiety

Anxiety is sticky,
a tenacious, toxic psychic glue,
highly communicable,
self-perpetuating,
expanding to conceal light,
waking fear and foreboding.

Faith and connection are antidotes,
memories of love and past miracles,
trust that darkness
carries its own gifts.
Paths to peace
offering acceptance.

Just routine

Routine oncology appointment
is a scary, misleading contradiction
despite a charming, flattering,
delightful doctor.

Bright pink elastic around my elbow
doesn't conceal blood was drawn
to check for tumor markers,
invisible harbingers of recurrence.

A peaceful cheerful room,
women in colorful scarves
quietly sitting in comfortable chairs
as chemical poisons drip in their arms.

Ours is a soft-spoken acceptance,
acquiescence born of necessity;
denial my gift, pending results,
quelling my urge to scream.

❋

Hospital bracelet

I've had my fourth and, if I'm very lucky,
last cancer–reconstruction surgery,
unwittingly expert in the patient dance,
joking with nurses and holding my daughter's hand.

Lessons in fear, acceptance, vulnerability and trust
wrapped in a small hospital bracelet
snapped on my wrist with confident finality
as my clothes are folded into a Patient Belongings Bag.

Condensed to my name, birthdate and case number
with a red companion bracelet listing allergies,
I repeat interminably the purpose of the surgery
and wonder if my stomach sounds as loud as it feels.

Though seldom cold, I begin to shiver,
teeth uncontrollably chattering,
as warm blankets are placed over my gown
and an intravenous portal to mysterious realms installed.

This poem was roaming through my mind last Friday
as I began the familiar pre-surgery minuet,
when the universe reminded me routine is an illusion,
as the bracelet was carefully locked onto my ankle.

Final surgery

My final surgery,
a glorious phrase,
cause for celebration.
Yet I'm unsettled, unsure, unfettered,
detached from cancer's leash,
acutely aware of my body
while floating above it,
acclimating to silence and space.

I participate in life,
recognizing isolation as an inside job,
drowning in feelings,
overflowing tears.
Poems a welcoming beacon,
as the tide of agitation subsides
leaving a transformed peace and balance,
emerging ballast of contentment.

Homecoming

Elixir of peace and contentment
walking in the front door
inhaling the garden
a cup of tea,
immersing in memories
waking in my own bed.
Solitude.
Home.

Tightrope

Struggling to balance,
honoring the facets of self,
Need for connection, love, empathy,
companionship, generosity;
balanced by cravings for observation,
solitude, beauty and poetry,
necessary to replenish and recharge my soul.

Physical aspects rise to the surface
as I heal after surgery;
time for rest, self care, asking for help,
struggling to release unreasonable expectations.
Learning to be without a task at hand,
aching for movement, action,
independence.

I imagine contradictions wearing smooth with time,
forming a sparkling, peaceful sphere,
but the edges remain sharp,
defaulting to their essential nature.
Distinct since my earliest memories,
so young, and needing others,
increasingly aware of a separate inner spirit.

Back on the edge

Good samaritan

Drove him down to the methadone clinic,
unwittingly entering a
surreal world.
Toddler incessantly crying,
squirming for escape.

Helpless metronome mom
swinging between pleading and threats.
Women shouting obscenities,
at each other, or imaginary foes.
Can't tell.

Desperate, agitated need.
Anger and fear
permeating the air.
Brief oases of silence
providing respite
where sanity can hide.

How could it be?

Embracing and nurturing illness
he finds himself disabled;

embracing and nurturing self pity
he finds himself a victim;

embracing and nurturing sadness
he finds himself depressed;

embracing and nurturing irresponsibility
he finds himself destitute;

embracing and nurturing chaos
he finds himself agitated;

embracing and nurturing addiction
he finds himself trapped;

embracing and nurturing ingratitude
he finds himself lacking;

embracing and nurturing entitlement
he finds himself alone;

looking around,
yet not within,

bewildered
at where he finds himself.

At peace

Alcohol killed him,
repeatedly cajoling
it would be one last time,
and it was.

Trumping love,
blocking his spirit's light,
the kind and decent person
concealed within.

Flying to Cindy

Snippets of conversation
Grandparents exchanging photos
and the merits of on-line dating.
A man lamenting a friend's
comment that he had
descended into resignation,
seemingly unaware that
acceptance is a blessing.

Inadequate distractions of my destination—
a hospital cradling my injured child,
holding my place
(her age irrelevant).
Overheard chatter teases my raw spirit
as the airplane transports me to a new reality.

Using tenuous boundaries
of closed eyes, books and tears,
grateful for conventions of solitude.
I embrace my fear and anxiety,
laughter and peace left behind,
as I feel the cold air of powerlessness.

ICU

Kindness, nurses, doctors,
indifference, bustle,
interminable ominous alarms
ignored by busy, determined people
focused on immediate tasks,
in a reality of emergencies
and the fragile thread of life.

Intravenous lines, a labyrinth of tubes,
unfamiliar machines monitored out of sight,
perhaps in a secret cave
by gnomes sipping chamomile,
appearing feasible
in this peculiar universe
of powerlessness and resignation.

Distraught families
bound by anxiety,
and the isolation of shuttered cell phones,
in a peculiar intimacy
based on shared experience,
as we retell the stories of our loved ones,
and recount trauma, gratitude and hope.

Eli

Mother and I were in the activities room
watching *I Love Lucy*
when a resident to her left said hello.
He asked me a lot of questions,
curious about our family,
and my nationality.

I smiled and answered each question,
trying to focus on my mother.
But he moved his wheelchair,
and sitting next to us,
continued his inquiries,
appearing fascinated by my responses.

He finally wheeled off
to the back of the room.
We grew tired of Lucy, so
I suggested the coffeeshop,
with its never ending supply
of cookies and bananas.

Mother nodded,
both of us accustomed
to one-sided conversations.
Did I just imagine
she looked amused
by the earlier exchange.

Struck by the sadness
of Eli's lucid mind
surrounded by confusion and silence,
I said goodbye to him as we passed,
but he had retreated to a secret private place
as he stared vacantly into space.

Forget Houdini

My mind is the master of distraction
when reality becomes painful,
creating an illusion of urgency
for absurd tasks.

I doubt I really must
buy salmon for dinner,
this minute,
when I already have too much food.

I question the necessity
of filing a medical claim,
today,
on Sunday.

I really don't want to think
my daughter lives on the edge
of a precipice,
blissfully unaware of mortality.

Mother has stopped eating,
and there's talk of hospice.
How much longer
can I evade acceptance.

126 ❧ Selma Mann

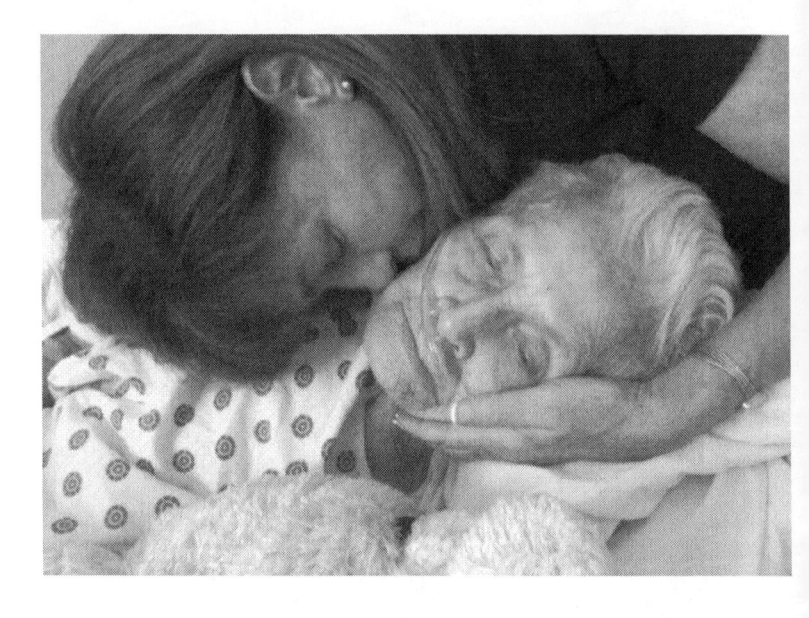

Ending

I see her winding down,
life slowing to basics,
as dreams of alternate dimensions
become her new reality.

Hospice care
bringing comfort and caring now,
with a timetable for peace
and graceful acceptance.

Grief on my sleeve

I'm wearing my grief on my sleeve,
again.
It was carefully packed
on my occasional-use shelf,
next to Algebra.

Mother's death
has made it part of my wardrobe,
again.

The grief is not as obvious
as after your sudden death, my love,
when I felt as if my spirit
had followed your soul,
eloping with it as your shadow.

A different loneliness has emerged
from the realization
that I'm an orphan now,
the newly-crowned family matriarch,
a stepping stone closer to the end.

Mortality feels closer
without Mother before me
shielding me from the night.

Transformations

Wonder

I wonder where butterflies go
when it rains,
I wonder where laughter goes
during tear storms,
I wonder where love goes
after death.

I wonder where peace goes
when I'm angry,
I wonder where trust goes
when I'm afraid.
I wonder where acceptance goes
when I try to control.

Are they all celebrating
in a mystical realm,
ephemeral,
immersed in spirit and beauty,
a place I can only visit
in dreams?

Transformation

I was so focused I couldn't see
wonders surrounding me.
Butterflies are, you know, portals to magic.
This morning on butterfly watch
I discovered black and gold caterpillars
industriously munching with tiny jaws.
They have faces
and lash-like antennas
as they transform greenery to beauty.
How could I not have noticed before.
Have they changed,
or have I?

Odd

I'm feeling odd,
singular,
a strange prime number
undivided in peculiar ways.
Life filled with connection
seems eerily irrelevant,
as my hand still feels
the phantom certainty
of yours.

I was part of a pair,
a soulmate,
temporary respite
on life's journey;
an unexpected
joyful distraction,
walking side by side,
honoring each other
as unique.

My soul has always been
a hermit with wings,
able to fly,
filled with light and love.

Gifts of awareness pour through me,
as poems illuminate
paths to my spirit,
a recurrent recognition
I am whole.

Falling

I had forgotten aimlessly pacing
around the house
after Al died.
Finding myself doing it again,
I walk to the seashore
looking for poems;
purposeful pacing.

I hear a stranger
saying to his companions,
"There's something magical about the sea."
I can't disagree.
It drew me to console my sadness,
salty from generations
of concentrated tears.

Distracted, I fall,
unhurt,
protected by guardian angels
reminding me to be mindful,
to be grateful for blessings,
aware of the missing ballast
of Mother's existence.

Let's keep it our little secret.
We wouldn't want anyone
who loves me
to worry,
or suspect that my grieving spirit
will be drifting for a while,
looking for an anchor.

Grief again

Grief again, so familiar.
Have I been wading in it
all along,
comforted by its gentle waves
lapping around my soul?

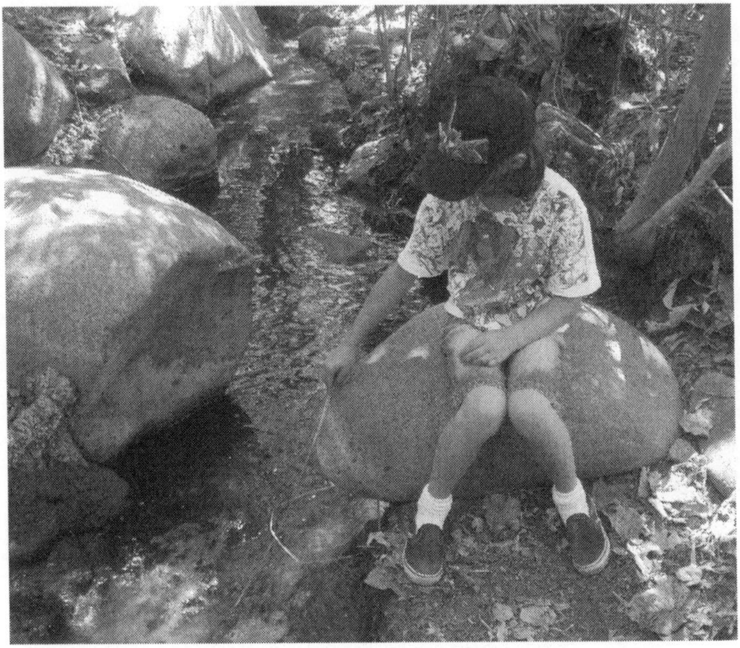

The care of love

Angels permit me
to help them tend my garden,
squeaky sparkling after rain,
whispering in my ear
that we could use
more flowering bushes,
alerting me to the impending emergence
of miraculous butterflies.
Garden Monarchs
appear to have decided to remain,
secure, loved and welcome,
forgoing perils of migration,
at least for now.

I'm allowed to tend to those I love too,
with frequent hugs,
a listening ear,
sharing pain and laughter,
sometimes just a "thinking of you" text,
as we acknowledge fear of loss,
remembering each other's stories,
honoring individuality,
weaving connection,
accepting the deceptively fragile web
that carries and links us,
bringing meaning and vulnerability,
handmaidens of love.

Dreaming

I've listened
in envious thrall
as friends describe
elaborate dreams
of flying, falling,
spiders spelunking,
childhood, and
visits from departed loves.

I seldom remember my own.
Snippets that tease me,
once in a long while,
before playfully disappearing
into my mind's
morning mist,
as they flee from my fruitless pursuit.

But sometimes my own smile wakes me.
What if I've been freely moving
between dimensions,
my unencumbered spirit
frolicking in adventures,
magical journeys unhampered
by the weight of translation,
since I won't remember.

Earring

Absurdly devastated by a lost earring
on the heels of a lost scarf
and of my favorite barrette,
the one with pictures of us,
laughing, not suspecting
the grief around the corner.

Earrings come in pairs,
reminders of our couple life.
As if I could forget
the third anniversary
of your death,
beginning life without you.

I can't wear just one.
It would be unbalanced, odd.
Yet I expect myself to smile,
focusing on gifts,
grateful for a poem,
feeling like a single earring.

Putter

Getting ready for a trip,
I putter.

Anxious and afraid,
I putter.

Pondering mortality,
I putter.

Restless and impatient,
I putter.

Uncertain about the future,
I putter.

It would appear
I have a putter default setting.

I've found the perfect meditation:
mindful puttering.

Folding laundry

Old pillowcases are the best,
worn by use and time,
smooth and cool against my cheek,
delicious;
all the more precious
because they won't last forever.

Mother is gone now.
Her cheek was smooth and cool,
cherished antique velvet,
fading,
responding to love and touch
until the end.

Passport

Waiting patiently in a drawer,
snuggled next to Al's,
my passport is ready for adventure.

It receives my sporadic thoughts
of places I have never been
tickling my spirit.

It feels my loyal presence
at French classes,
seemingly without purpose.

I sense it smiling now,
as the possibilities
move toward reality;

plans set aside for years,
gears grudgingly engaging,
as vision clears.

Imaginary voyages
awaken love of travel,
after all.

Beautiful baby girl

Beautiful baby girl,
a dark-haired pixie with a one-sided grin,
your wide blue eyes look us over
not missing a thing.
A wave of overwhelming love,
catches me by surprise,
bearing a primordial need
to keep you safe from harm.

Nurses insist you're far too young to smile,
but it sure looks like you mean it.
Already, you have a mind of your own,
coming into the world feet first,
refusing the conventional entry.
I wouldn't be surprised to hear
you were trying to get a running start on life,
your perfect, fragile fingers already tugging at my heart.

Friends look at my brown eyes and predict
that your blue ones will soon change to mirror mine.
But you will see the world with blue-green eyes
that will reflect the colors surrounding you.
Predictable only in your unpredictability,
you never cease to surprise, challenge and delight,
as long as you know I'm somewhere nearby,
the only hint of your vulnerable spirit.

Creation

I thought I was finished
with gestation periods,
having delivered
two beautiful baby girls
in another century,
my body becoming
creation's vessel;
until grief, loss, illness,
fear and pain
wrenched out
my muse
with her treasure trove,
bearing poetry.

Edge

I've been trying to talk myself off the edge,
when maybe, instead, it's time for dancing there.

If my head starts to warn of potential downfalls,
we could just sit there, admiring the view,
befriending butterflies, angels and poems,
until we hear the music and are ready to move on.

You see, that's where the excitement lies,
and it's the perfect place to take a leap of faith.

About the poet

Selma Mann was born in Barquisimeto, Venezuela to Julius and Carlota. Julius was a German Jew who emigrated after Hitler came to power; Carlota an orphan with an indomitable will to transcend. Their legacy to Selma has proved to be a joyful, positive attitude, compassion and a love of learning. Her early education was by austere yet caring nuns as the only Jewish student at a Barquisimeto Catholic school until she was joined by her younger sister Lili.

Immigrating to the United States when she was 11, Selma's family found its way to West Los Angeles. Already bilingual, speaking her native Spanish as well as German, Selma's English was mostly self-taught, mainly through long, daily stretches of reading at the small local library. This became the foundation for a couple of life-long habits: time, money and energetic support of public libraries, and a passion for languages. She has since added Italian and French to her repertoire.

She practiced public law for 27 years beginning her legal career at Rutan & Tucker before landing at the City of Anaheim. Prior to becoming an attorney, Selma thoroughly enjoyed teaching gifted second and third graders in Culver City for over 11 years. This proved to be the ideal occupation while raising two spirited young daughters, Cindy and Laurie.

Inveterate and leisurely world travelers, Selma and her late husband Al took equal pleasure in discovering new cities as in returning to known favorites, including a half-dozen cruises to Alaska and multiple voyages to Paris, London, Florence and Venice, Bruges—"really old and full of chocolate"—Vancouver and Hong Kong—"best dim sum"—Vitoria Gasteiz and Kyoto, as well as beloved stateside getaways.

Earlier tastes in poetry tended toward the traditional: Shakespeare's sonnets, John Donne, John Milton, Elizabeth Barrett Browning, and Dylan Thomas. But Billy Collins, reading and lecturing at the Newport Beach public library opened her eyes and ears to wider possibilities for poetic expression. Struck by Collins' joy in his poetry, Selma has since found writing poetry more a pleasure than a labor. This augurs well for future production, very well indeed.

She is currently working on a second collection of poems.

Not so secret vices: chocolate and puttering.

❖

selmajmann@gmail.com

Mourning Cloak

Text   Adobe Jenson Pro 12.5/14
Section Titles   Mr. Bedfort

Widgets, doojammers, and dingbats
        Butterflies
        Illustries
        Gargoyles of France
        Adobe Wood Type Ornaments
        Adobe Caslon Pro
        WasWoodcuts

Typeset in Adobe InDesignCS
Photo Work in GIMP and PhotoshopCS

Designed for Premiere Sortie Press by
Jabungus Int'l
Santa Barbara, California
2013